For Joa

best wishes

Ranjit

THE ART OF TRANSLATION

Ranjit Bolt

The Art Of Translation

OBERON BOOKS

LONDON

First published in 2010 by Oberon Books Ltd

521 Caledonian Road, London N7 9RH

Tel: 020 7607 3637 / Fax: 020 7607 3629

e-mail: info@oberonbooks.com

www.oberonbooks.com

A catalogue record for this book is available from the British Library.

ISBN: 978-1-84002-865-2

Printed in Great Britain by CPI Antony Rowe, Chippenham

Contents

For Mum and Dad

Preface

T HIS BOOK DOES venture, occasionally, into "high-brow" territory (Dryden, Walter Benjamin, et al) but it is not intended to be a profoundly theoretical, intellectual analysis of the art of translation. Indeed, I would prefer to call it the *business* of translation, the more so as that is exactly what translation has *been,* for me, over the past twenty years or so – a way of earning a living. These are, then, notes from the coalface – the observations – the accumulated (Gawd 'elp us) "wisdom", of someone who, after a decade of safe, monthly remunerated employment, found himself suddenly cast, through a concatenation of good luck (Jonathan Miller's doing my version of *Le Menteur* at the Old Vic) and lunacy, into the troubled waters of freelance translation – a perilous field at the best of times, but I suspect never more perilous, precarious, than in the theatre.

I first began to think seriously about what it meant to be a translator after a temporary falling out with a close friend. It was all to do with status, I suppose, and ego. Not a nice admission to have to make. I was in the Groucho Club with a couple of friends and a young, attractive actress showed up, as young attractive actresses have a habit of doing at the Groucho Club, and during the course of conversation, during which I had been unaccustomedly silent, she turned to me and asked me what I "did".

Now, as it happened, this was a question I had lately been asking myself. I had had something on at the National Theatre, a "translation", I use the quotation marks advisedly – well, the quotation marks are the whole point of this chapter, if not of this book; anyway, what I'd had on was a *version* – yes, let's call it a version, much safer word – of Brecht's awful play, perhaps the worst he ever wrote, *The Resistible Rise Of Arturo Ui*. I'd made a creditable fist of this. In fact, Malcolm Rutherford, in the Financial Times, had hailed me as "the translator as star" and the novelist and critic Howard Jacobson had announced (on the BBC, so it had to be true) that "the translator, Ranjit Bolt, is now a star in his own right."[1]

The point of this trumpet-blowing is to highlight something about the role of the translator. Rutherford's remark evinced surprise, as who would say: "Gosh! Here's a translator who makes one sit up and take notice of him!", while Jacobson's suggested that one can be a translator while at the same time being something more. The translator, of course, is the first person to want to believe this. When you're sitting in a prestigious theatre, watching one of your *versions* being performed, and a thousand odd people are laughing at regular intervals, the temptation

– one is only human, after all – is to take credit for as much of the laughter as possible. After all, the thing is in English now – in my case, often rhyming couplets, at that – and the English, and the rhymes, are yours, not Moliere's or Corneille's or whosoe'er it be. It's a heady feeling that you get from that audience response, and it's only human – humanly arrogant, let's say – to want to lay claim to as much of it as possible. If there's "no such thing as translation", as sundry theorists would have us believe, then to some extent every translation is a re-writing, and every translator, for better or worse, a writer. But more of that anon, in Chapter Two to be precise, and back now to the Groucho Club.

So there I was, sipping my rioja, hastily debating with myself what answer I should give to this, as I say extremely sexy, young actress. Translator didn't feel to be the way to go. Bit of a passion-killer. In fact, I might as well have said chartered accountant. So I plumped for writer. "I'm a writer," I heard myself say out loud, and she seemed suitably impressed.

"No you're not," said a voice to my right (a voice belonging to the aforementioned close friend), "you're a translator."

I was livid. In the heat of wounded vanity I didn't speak to the guy for a week. He had "trodden on my dreams", as Yeats would have put it, and shoved me rudely back into the dry, prosaic, transatorial box from which, for fifteen minutes, believing my own press, I thought I'd escaped. Or he had if he was right. But was he? I think not.

As long as you're not translating a laundry list, or an Ikea assembly booklet, or something of that nature, it's very hard, and probably not desirable, for a translator to be just that – a flat, invisible *renderer* of meanings. In pretty much any other context, a translator is more than that, and that is something he, or she – and we, the reader – should embrace. The creative translator should not be rapped over the knuckles (as I have been on numerous occasions) for being too conspicuous. There is really no such thing as a good translation that is not, to a greater or lesser extent, creative. The tag "creative translator" is, in fact, a tautology, at any rate in the context of what is known as "literary translation", and it is exclusively that genre that I shall be looking at in this study, as the title *The Art of Translation* obviously implies.

I question whether literary translators may actually lay claim to the exalted status accorded them by Walter Benjamin, in his essay *The Task of the Translator* (of which more later), but if anyone is in any doubt that we have at least some part to play, I would merely mention what happened to the late, great Simon Gray, when a production of a play of his was put on by a German theatre company. Half way through the performance a character entered covered from head to foot in an enormous orthopaedic cast. Simon turned, in bewilderment, to the director, who was sitting next to him, and asked him what the Hell was going on. (Presumably, he imagined, this was some sort of surreal, Teutonic flourish.) "But it says in the text," the director replied, "that this character is 'completely plastered throughout the scene.'"

1. Vive L'Impossibilité!

IN THE PAST, when I was asked to write (for talks, programme notes, etc.) about the art of literary translation, I would employ the metaphor of a leaky pitcher. Translating, I maintained, was like taking a leaky pitcher (the target language) to a well (the original text, the host language) and trying to transport water (the original meaning, or content) in it to a bath or basin (the speakers and readers of the target language, or audiences, in my case). It was a better analogy than I at first realised, because of course the word "translation", coming, as it does, from the Latin word "transfero" actually contains within it the idea of carrying something across from one place, language, to another.

No matter how hard you tried, so I maintained, a certain quantity of the water – the original content, in other words – would inevitably be lost. I realize now, after two decades spent at the translational coalface, that this metaphor won't quite do. It is fundamentally misleading, because it suggests that there is an x – the "meaning" or "content" of the original – that is somehow to be transported, albeit imperfectly, but as intact as possible, in the pitcher of translation.

If you start out, as a literary translator... Let me break off for a moment... From now on – or at any rate very shortly – I shall be omitting the word "literary" to save space, but it should be assumed that it is always that branch of translation that I am discussing. Obviously it is eminently possible to translate a shopping list, a technical manual, anything of that nature, without losing any of its content or meaning at all, or, unless one makes some silly slip, adding anything of one's own. But if you start out, as a *literary* translator, with the view of your function just outlined, you are doomed to failure from the outset.

My pitcher analogy is not wholly invalid. Insofar as it contains the idea of some sort of inherent inadequacy in the translation process – of something we might think can be achieved by it, but which in fact cannot – it is barking up the right tree. But the image of pitcher and water still clings to the idea of something – an x – a "meaning" or "sense" – having to be transferred from one language to another, and from foreign writer to, in my case, English audience. The sad fact is that, in a very meaningful sense, there simply *is* no such x – no such *paraphrasable content*, to use that technical expression again – that literary translation so conveys. All translators, and anyone thinking about translation, must begin by accepting this premise – they must, if you like, experience this epiphany.

To make the point a little clearer, let us consider the precepts set out by the sixteenth century translator and thinker Étienne Dolet in his seminal work on the subject, *Le Maniere de Bien Traduire d'Une Langue en l'Autre*. One of Dolet's key stipulations is that the translator should have a perfect understanding, not merely of the substance of a the text he is translating, but also of its author's *intention*. The trouble is that, as we all know in this post-intentionalist fallacy era, the intention of the author of a literary text is by no means necessarily the same thing as the actual meaning, or meanings (let us not forget the modern obsession with polyvalence) of that text. The meaning of a literary text is, to put it a touch flippantly, up for grabs, and up for grabs with it goes the strategy to be employed by its translator.

I would go further and argue that, never mind the original author's *intention*, one can think of instances – of specific texts – where it may not even be necessary for a literary translator to have any knowledge of the *language* he or she is translating from. Which, for example, would you rather read: a translation of *The Divine Comedy* by a brilliant Italian scholar with no poetic gift, or one by a brilliant poet with no knowledge of Italian, working from a literal version? Lorca, the great Spanish translator of Shakespeare, might have agreed with this. At any rate, his famous observation about translating Shakespeare is certainly consistent with it. When asked how he coped with the Elizabethan English, he replied: "The problem isn't my English – it's my Spanish!" Carry that statement to its logical extreme and you arrive at the possibility of a great translation of a great work of literature being possible by someone with no knowledge of the language it was written in, and nothing but an accurate crib to go on.

But to return to the main issue: the so to speak "impossibility" of literary translation. The mistake is to view this discovery – epiphany, as I have called it – as something depressing. It can just as easily be seen as positive and liberating. According to legend, while Proust was writing *A La Recherche du Temps Perdu*, and Scott Moncrief was, at the same time, bringing out his famous translation, it became fashionable among certain Parisian intellectuals to await the Moncrief version of each successive volume, rather than read the original, the idea being that Moncrief had, in some sense, done Proust better than Proust did himself. This is an extreme example, and perhaps an apocryphal one to boot, but I am happy to report it here because for me, whether it actually happened or not, it conveys a kernel of truth. Granted, Moncrief's translation will never convey to an English reader the full experience (insofar as there is something peculiarly French about it, and isolable as such – itself a moot point) that a French reader has while reading Proust in the original. (And remember, what I am maintaining here is that the reason it cannot do this is nothing to with any shortcomings on Moncrief's part, but simply because such a feat is inherently impossible.) But that needn't necessarily mean that Moncrief's version is instantly and necessarily doomed to the status of a poor second best, or unhappy compromise. It is possible for a translator to achieve great things, and to render sterling service to the original author and text, even if there is no such thing as translation in some complete, or exhaustive sense.

To summarise what I have been saying so far: we start with a descriptive proposition. There is no such thing as a complete, one hundred per cent "accurate", or "faithful" translation, or perhaps even anything close to it. The notion of absolute fidelity is a fallacy, a chimera that will never be realized if we translate from now till doomsday. From that *descriptive* proposition, a second, *prescriptive* one follows: do not *strive* for what can never be achieved; do not set your sites on complete fidelity, when there is no such thing, or you will only tie yourself in knots.

And here comes the twist – the positive aspect of what appears, *prima facie*, to be a discouraging discovery. From this second, prescriptive proposition – don't aim for the unattainable – there follows the idea of an acceptable degree of licence. Because the myth of total fidelity is just that – a myth – you are not only entitled, but perhaps even *obliged,* as a translator, to allow yourself some measure of freedom. Once you have accepted this, you have given yourself at least a fair chance of doing a good job. The degree of licence required, and or allowed, will vary from author to author and from text to text. With a difficult text, some degree of licence may be essential if one is to get anywhere at all. With a mediocre text, some degree of licence may be enticing, as an opportunity to provide one's reader or audience with something better than the original. Sometimes, again, a text may be both so relatively transparent and so major that licence is neither necessary nor justifiable. And so on and so forth in varying shades and permutations. Moreover, there is nothing to prevent different approaches – i.e. more or less free – being adopted by different translators of the same text, and them all achieving good results. Russian friends tell me that Tolstoy loses (whatever that word "loses" means) relatively little in translation, whereas Dostoyevsky loses quite a lot, and Pushkin more or less all. As to what is meant by "loses", I suppose it must have something to do with the *reading experience* which a Russian gets when he or she reads the work. Presumably not just any Russian reader, either, but a more or less intelligent, sensitive one. A good translation will come as close as possible to recreating that experience for its own readers. From this, if it is true, I imagine it must follow that the translator of Tolstoy needs, and is permitted, the minimum degree of licence, and the translator of Pushkin the maximum. In French, my own speciality, I would suggest that Balzac, say, loses relatively little in translation, while, at the opposite end of the spectrum, I, for one, can barely imagine what it might mean to "translate" Baudelaire or Mallarmé at all. Interestingly, these last two, and Pushkin too, are poets, and, as the famous adage has it: poetry is what is lost in translation. But obviously the same thing applies to prose: one has only to think of Shakespeare, say, or Joyce, in *Ulysses* at any rate, to say nothing of *Finnegan's Wake*, to see that that must be true.

The Earl of Roscommon, in his *Essay On Translated Verse,* articulates some of these points without recourse to technical terminology, but with beautiful clarity. The overzealous pursuer of accuracy, he points out, is shooting himself in the foot. He will only "grow unjust by seeming overnice/For superstitious virtue turns to vice." Implicit in that paradox of virtue turning to vice is the observation I began with: that fidelity is, in some fundamental, overarching sense, an impossibility – a seductive, destructive chimera. Roscommon had grasped an essential truth of translation and expressed it as succinctly, perhaps, as any writer ever has. "Try to be as faithful as you can," he says, "but for God's sake don't forget to be good!" Loss of literary quality is too high a price to pay for an unbending closeness to the original. Granted, Roscommon is here speaking about the translation of poetry in particular, but his point applies, to a greater or lesser extent, to the novel and to drama also. Small wonder that one of the greatest translators of all time, Dryden, should so have admired Roscommon's poem:

> Yet modestly he does his work survey
> And calls a finished poem an "essay";
> For all the needful rules are scattered here
> Truth smoothly told, and pleasantly severe;
> (So well is Art disguised, for Nature to appear.)
> Nor need those rules, to give translation light,
> His own example is a flame so bright
> That he who but arrives to copy well
> Unguided will advance, unknowing will excel.[2]

In his Preface to his translations of Ovid, Dryden, copying Ancient Greek theorists, outlines three different types of translation. The first is "metaphrase" – "word for word" as we might say, or "verbum pro verbo", to use Cicero's formulation. Cicero deplores this method of translation and Dryden follows him. By "metaphrase" Dryden means the sort of pedantic, slavish, "overnice" adherence to the original which Roscommon, as we just saw, condemns.

There is further authority for this rejection of literalism in Horace. "Nor" he writes in the *Ars Poetica,* "must you be so faithful a translator, as to take the pains of rendering the original word for word; nor by imitating throw yourself into straits, whence either shame or the rules of your work may forbid you to retreat." Once again, an overzealous adherence to the original is discouraged, and by an expert imitator as well as poet.

Dryden's second category is "paraphrase", or "translation with latitude", as he also calls it – latitude being, of course, his word for what we would most probably call licence. The third category – what Dryden terms "imitation", and we should probably call adaptation – need not concern us here.

Dryden's conclusion, or at any rate the one he draws in his preface to his translations of Pindar, is that what one should aim for is some sort of happy medium. A good translation will, in Dryden's opinion, be neither so loose as paraphrase, nor so close as metaphrase. The interesting point here is that, with the instinct and common sense of a highly intelligent man, coupled to the experience of a skilled practitioner, Dryden has, implicitly and unconsciously, arrived at the same conclusion that the modern linguistic theorist reaches by more technical means, through the denial of a paraphrasable content. The acceptance of a linguistic-philosophical truth leads logically to the adoption of a somewhat, but not excessively, relaxed code of practice. It is this central premise, and its consequences, as instantiated by various translations through the ages, that shall form the nub of this short study. And one of my key findings will I hope be that the impossibility of truly faithful translation – the absurdity, even, of such a concept – far from being a handicap, can actually be a boon to the translator.

Nor, by the same token, is a sort of *literary reverence* for the original always a virtue. Consider, for instance, Dryden's attitude to Chaucer, of whom he, somewhat condescendingly, writes, in his preface to *Fables Ancient and Modern*: "If I have altered him anywhere for the better, I must at the same time acknowledge, that I could have done nothing without him."[3] Interestingly, in the same essay, Dryden echoes Roscommon in his use (again in connection with Chaucer) of the word "superstition", to denote an excessive and unhelpful reverence for the original. "When an ancient word, for its sound and significancy, deserves to be revived, I have that reasonable veneration for anitquity, to restore it. All beyond is superstition."[4]

In a similar vein, Pope, in his preface to his translation of *The Iliad,* tempers his reverence for Homer with a certain measure of patronization, describing his work as "a wild paradise, where, if we cannot see all the beauties so distinctly as in an ordered garden, it is only because the number of them is infinitely greater... If some things are too luxuriant it is owing to the richness of the soil; and if others are not arrived to perfection and maturity, it is only because they are overrun and oppressed by those of a stronger nature."[5] Speaking of Homer's blemishes (and the implication is that these are neither few nor inconsiderable) he remarks that we "admire even while we disapprove. Nay, where this" (Homer's sublimity) "appears, though attended with absurdities, it brightens the rubbish about it." All this may not quite be damning with faint praise, and it is worth pointing out that the same translator once remarked that he found himself "utterly incapable of doing justice to Homer", but the admiration herein expressed is certainly to some degree ambivalent. The taking of some liberties may not actually be a corollary of this attitude of Pope's toward his original, but it is certainly likely. And such an approach would of course tie in very nicely with Dryden's theory of a midpoint between metaphrase and paraphrase, which has already been described, and which we shall examine, in the next chapter, being put into practice by both Dryden and Pope, those two classical giants both of poetry and of literary translation.

2. C'est Magnifique, Mais...

A T THE RISK of overegging my Dryden pudding, the great man also remarks, in his Preface to his translation of the *Sylvae*, that "A translator is to make his author appear as charming as possibly he can, provided he maintains his character." By the author's "character", of course, Dryden means what we would call, to use a hackneyed phrase, "the spirit of the original". The interesting point here is the implied tension between the translation being entertaining – well written, in fact – on the one hand, and faithful, on the other. This is the equivalent of the famous phrase coined by a seventeenth century French critic writing on translation, in which he compares translations to women, and describes good translations as: "les belles infidéles"[6] – "the fickle beauties." The implication, both of this and Dryden's observation, is that, to some extent, beauty, charm – whatever you want to call it – and accuracy are incompatible. Some sort of compromise is inevitable. A balance must be struck between litearay merit in the target language, and fidelity to the host language.

Not all great intellectuals have subscribed to this doctrine. When the great classicist Bentley met Pope, the great translator, who had just brought out his masterpiece version of *The Iliad*, he twitted him with the famous apophthegm: "A very pretty poem, Mr Pope, but is it Homer?" Evidentally Bentley, while acknowledging Pope's poetic facility – "prettiness" – found this to be more a hindrance than a help. Interesting that Bentley actually used the same word – "pretty", "belle" – as that French critic I just quoted, and perhaps with the same implication: namely, that there is an inherent conflict between literary quality and fidelity.

We revere the ancients less these days than our forebears, of course, nor is that necessarilt a bad thing. It is true, as Eliot points out in his essay *What Is A Classic*, that if we know more than the authors of the past, they are what we know. However, that, on its own, doesn't make them great, any more than, if all I had in the larder was a can of baked beans and a packet of sliced bread, then baked beans on toast would be a great dish. If I had been present at that now legendary clash between the eminent scholar and the great poet, I would probably have chipped in, in Pope's defence, with the obvious retort: "No, Sir, and 'tis the better for it," or something suitably eighteenth century along those lines.

Pope himself, as we have seen, had an ambivalent attitude towards Homer, a mixture of reverence and condescension, but he certainly would not have dared to suggest – or at any rate, not in public – that he had actually *improved* on his original. Shockingly enough, though, in many ways he had. If you weigh Pope's version of *The Iliad* against the original you will find that, line for line, it is probably a better poem. It is written in some of the smoothest, most sonorous and technically perfect verse any human being has ever produced. It made its author a rich man, and rightly so. On the other hand, Bentley was right – it's not Homer.

You pays your money and you takes your choice. Pope would have been incapable of reproducing the earthy tragedy, the primeval, gut-wrenching unsentimentality, that Homer achieves in Book Twenty-Four of *The Iliad* – the episode in which Priam comes to Achilles' tent to reclaim the body of his dead son, Hector. This (Book Twenty-Four, that is, not the whole *Iliad)* is, for my money, the first unquestionably great poem in Western literature. And there is something basic, visceral, in it that Pope not merely fails to replicate, but was congenitally, as a poet, incapable of capturing.

When Achilles urges the grief-shattered Priam to eat some supper he uses the analogy of Niobe. In Greek mythology, Niobe's children were struck down by Hera as a punishment for boasting that she was more fertile than the goddess Leto, in that she had twelve children – six sons and six daughters – to Leto's paltry one of each, albeit the one each in question were Apollo and Artemis. As a punishment for her conceit, Leto ordered Artemis to shoot to death Niobe's daughters, and Apollo to dispatch her sons by the same MO. Niobe wept solidly, and abstained from food, for nine days, but on the tenth she could hold out no longer, but dried her tears and broke her fast. It is a brilliant, almost Joycean assertion of life, humanity, vulnerability, over romantic and impossible idealism, and Homer captures its significance in a single immortal line:

He d'ara sitou mnesat', epei kamë dakru cheousa

"And then Niobe thought she might eat something, for she was tired of weeping."[7]

Astonishingly, Pope doesn't merely fail to capture this earthiness. He leaves the line out entirely. Presumably it does not fit in with his Augustan view of human nature. But had he translated it, his style would not have been up to the job. He could never have reached the gut in the way Homer does. He was, quite simply, too good – or, to put it another way, too effortlessly, but also unremittingly, elegant. And this elegance, this sheer, technical and tonal smoothness, can have unfortunate consequences.

For instance, in his translation of Book Twenty-Three, when Pope comes to the prize for the wrestling contest in Patroclus' funeral games, he renders:

> "and for the loser, a woman, a skilled one, valued at four (oxen)"[8]

thus:

> And next, the loser's spirits to restore,
> A female captive valued but at four.[9]

There is an elegance, a wit, almost a flippancy, in the Pope that simply isn't there in the Homer. This bears Bentley out: it is touches, changes, like these which, along with the smoothness of the versification, make Pope's version a very different poem from Homer's. But as to its being an inferior one, surely wit and elegance are poetic virtues? So, on balance, Pope wins, though there are moments where he falls short, or ducks the challenge altogether. Both these aspects – his overall triumph and his occasional shortcomings – tell us something about the nature of literary translation, about how, if poetry is what is lost in translation, it can also, in the right hands, be what is gained.

The same thing happens in Dryden's *Aeneid*. For instance, Virgil's immortal:

> Infandum regina iubes renovare dolorem[10]
> Queen, you order me to renew unspeakable pain

is rendered as:

> Great queen, what you command me to relate
> Renews the sad remembrance of our fate[11]

"Remembrance" is wrong. The idea of remembrance is contained in "renew". Also, Dryden gives us two lines where Virgil has only one, thus losing the lapidary quality of the verse. But what the translator loses in these respects he more than regains in elegance and sonority, while the brilliance of his technique – his mastery of rhyme and rhythm – as with Pope, enlivens what would otherwise be, page for page, rather a dreary read. Johnson seems to have regarded rhyming verse, on the page, at any rate, as, in some key sense, preferable, even superior, to blank,[12] and I'm inclined to agree with him. Shakespeare didn't write blank verse to be read. I suspect he would have thought the idea absurd. His never bothering to collate his plays in a published edition implies that. By the same token, both Dryden and Pope, in their great translations, indisputably, bring something to the party – something beautiful and enhancing: a technical mastery of an inherently diverting medium, the rhyming couplet.

For the last two decades I have spent a good deal of my life translating French comedies – particularly the verse comedies of Molière and Corneille – using a sort of low-grade, pragmatic version of the medium employed with such imperious, effortless skill by the two giants I've been looking at in this chapter. If there is one thing I have learnt during that time it is that theatrical tastes have changed. It is a fact that must be admitted that, line for line, Molière is not a funny writer. His comedy is almost exclusively either psychological or situational, rather than verbal. It is therefore permissible for, if not incumbent upon, his modern-day translators to tweak and change in an effort to extract extra humour from what would otherwise be, line for line, sometimes rather dreary dialogue. This is what translators and adaptors such as Richard Wilbur, Tony Harrison, Martin Crimp, and the author, have endeavoured to do.

For example, Corneille's and Molière's audiences would have relished long, rhetoric-laiden speeches. Such *tours de force* would have drawn from their original hearers gasps of appreciation and bursts of applause like the cries of "Wah wah!" that routinely punctuate poetic recitations on the subcontinent. Take, for example, the homilies that Molière puts into the mouths of his raisonneurs (English:

THE ART OF TRANSLATION

"reasoners" or "arguers") – common-sense figures who propound the sane and balanced viewpoint that, it is probably safe to say, is more or less Molière's own. To a present-day audience, these set pieces can veer dangerously close to tediousness at times, and can also appear ham-fisted from a dramatic point of view, as well as theatrically inept. Modern English and American audiences, reared on a faster, wise-cracking brand of verbal comedy, will not stomach these speeches in an un-diluted, or -adapted, form. At some point – be it stage one, during the initial translation process, or stage two, during rehearsals, or even, if one is caught napping, stage three, during previews – the scissors will, more often than not, have to come out, and probably the pen too.

In general, cuts to the works of such second division playwrights as Racine, Corneille, Marivaux and Molière (I speak of the French because they are what I know best, not because I would wish to suggest that they are especially at fault) are a theatrical necessity, and you ignore that necessity at your peril. It simply does not do to allow oneself to be burdened with the baggage of a tradition that has made demi-gods out of mere mortals, and to regard every line they write as sacred and unexcisable. If this seems outrageous – sacrilegious, even – only stop to consider how directors will today routinely cut a masterpiece such as *Hamlet* or *King Lear*, without a qualm.

Few if any playwrights, and very few plays, are uncuttable. To this day I wince when I recall the three and a half hour long first preview of a production of Brecht's *The Resistible Rise of Arturo Ui,* for which I did the translation. We lost the audience distressingly early on in the proceedings and we never got them back, or if we did, then only in fits and starts. We had committed the cardinal sin of regarding one of the worst plays of a major playwright as not to be tampered with (or not enough) simply because it was *by* who it was by. We had failed to take into account the fact that Brecht wrote the play in haste in three weeks while waiting to leave Europe for America. I can only add that when the scissors did come out, which they did, with alacrity, there was a collective sigh of relief all (well, pretty much all)[13] round, which is saying something, given how reluctant actors are to part with even one line, let alone a whole chunk of them.

And just as cuts are often permissible, if not essential, so additions, within due bounds, can be welcome too, and need not be viewed as an immediate crossing of the boundary between translation and adaptation. One swallow doesn't make a summer, and one or two liberties here and there don't make an outrage. One incident that will always remain etched on my memory, occurred during a production of *Tartuffe* that I did in the West End in 1991. Nick Le Prevost, an excellent actor who had found himself saddled with the role of Cleante, the raissonneur, soon found himself to be the only actor in the show who was not getting a single laugh. All he had to do was spout long speeches propounding the sensible view of every situation that arose during the play. After a few nights of this he came to me, more or less tearing his hair, and pleaded with me to write in a laugh for him – just one good one would do – so that he would know, during the evening, that it was on its way, and that the audience were going to get their comeuppance for not laughing at him before. I managed to come up with a gag that in fact earned him the best laugh of the evening. It was a potent illustration of the fact that sticking rigidly to the original text can be death.

Furthermore, one can respect, even revere, the playwright one is translating, while still giving oneself permission to interfere, now and then, with his or her text. There is more than one way to skin this particular cat. There are also subtler methods than the one I employed for Nick, of simply inserting material for which there is no equivalent in the original. What one might call creative translation can just as successfully add a bit of zip to the dialogue, as and when it would seem to be required. One of the couplets in my 2002 National Theatre translation of *Tartuffe* that elicited much favourable comment from critics occurred during the scene in which Tartuffe, while

Orgon hides under the table, is attempting to have is way with Elmire in Act Four. The French goes as follows:

ELMIRE:
> Et l'on ne peut aller jusqu'à vous satisfaire,
> Qu'aux dernières faveurs on ne pousse l'affaire?[14]

Literal translation:
> Can one not satisfy you except by going to the limit of (i.e. sexual) favours?

My translation went like this:
> And now you're rushing to the sweet
> Before we've had the soup and meat.

That last couplet was always greeted with a tremendous laugh. But what really pleased me about this was that although that laugh wasn't there in the French, in order to achieve it I hadn't really *tampered* with the text at all, I had simply *translated* it in a way that rendered it funnier than it was in the French.

Here is another example of this type of creative translation – embellishment, but with a legitimate basis in the original text, from my translation of Corneille's *Le Menteur:*

LUCRECE:

C'est bien aimer la fourbe, et l'avoir bien en main

Car pour moi, plus j'y songe, et moins j'y puis comprendre

Quel fruit auprès de vous il en ose prétendre.[15]

Literal translation:

He really is fond of deceit, and has it down to a fine art. As for me, the more I think about it, the less I understand it. Does he really expect to curry favour with you by lying like this?

This came out (somewhat freely, I have to admit, but nonetheless with sufficient basis in the French) as:

Why did he bother spouting all that tosh?

He surely must have known it wouldn't wash;

He lies to everybody, willy-nilly,

Whoever heard of anything so stupid?

The last couplet always earned a terrific laugh, but again, it has to be said, the laugh had nothing to do with the original. It was the variation on the old gag: "There once was a girl from St Pauls/Who grabbed a young man by the hair" that brought the house down. I remember putting the couplet in during technical rehearsals. A technician was at work up in the lighting rig above the stage. When the willy-nilly/stupid couplet came, I heard him chuckle. I knew I'd struck gold, and that chuckle was going to be magnified a thousandfold, in a day or two's time, into a show-stopping laugh. So it proved. Was Corneille – great *homme de theatre* that he was, looking down from on high and frowning? Somehow I rather doubt it.

I have been sticking in this chapter to what I know best – French verse comedy – but it goes without saying that the same rules apply to translating plays in any language, and be it in verse or prose. If a joke occurs to the translator that is neither out of keeping with the spirit of the original, nor unduly subverts the text, then I, for one, see no point in not putting it in. Whether Molière, Corneille, or whose'er it be, would have condoned such practice is a moot point, but fortunately they are no longer here to argue the toss, while, in the meantime, audiences go home that bit happier.

What I have been saying really all amounts to an attempt to refute the old Italian saying: "Traduttore, Tradittore!" – "Translator, traitor." This expression is, if you like, the other side of the "belles infidéles" coin. The Italian phrase deplores what the French critic advocates, or at least admits has its good side: a judicious licence in the service of good literature. But both phrases have the same basic import: there is something inherent in the translation process that leads, inexorably, towards licence. One appears to lament this fact. The other, while perhaps not wholly pleased by it, at least admits that it has its positive side. But both at least accept it as inevitable.

A translator simply *cannot* help diverging from the original to some degree. As with Pope's attitude to Homer, or Dryden's to Chaucer, undue reverence is to be eschewed. To take an example from my own field of expertise, the English translator of Molière has an illustrious comic tradition in his own language to tell him just where Molière stands in the pantheon of comic playwrights. He is good, yes – very good indeed – but he is not great. In particular, looking at our own, British counterparts, his theatrical sense is arguably not so fine as that of Wycherley, say, or Congreve, or Sheridan, while his wit and intelligence are indubitably less. His English translators should bear this in mind on commencing their work. There are authors whose somewhat lower stature permits a more creative literary translator to view an original text as not unlike a swimming pool on a hot day where he or she can splash about a bit, just so long as they don't pee in the water.

I have got into trouble more than once for my cavalier approach to the business of translating those great French theatrical behemoths, Molière and Corneille. One critic wrote in *The Times*, of my translation of Molière's *Les Femmes Savantes,* that I should be: "taken to the top

of the tallest tower in the City" (I was working as an
investment manager at the time) "and thrown off it"[16] as
a fitting punishment for presuming – and I a City slicker
of all things – to tamper with the work of the mighty
Molière. Charles Spencer, on the other hand, reviewing
my translation of *Tartuffe*, when it was performed at the
Royal National Theatre in 2002, wrote: "I, for one, have
never understood what all the fuss concerning Molière was
about. Fortunately Ranjit Bolt seems to share my view."[17]
For Spencer, irreverence was, it seemed, a virtue. Such are
the ever-baffling vagaries of critics, who contradict one
another, and themselves, for that matter, at every turn.

One should not start out, then, with some sort of lierary,
or translatorial inferiority complex. Still sticking to my own
field, the translation of seventeenth century French verse
comedies, my approach has always been that if poetry,
as the famous adage goes, is what is lost in translation,
then it is also, or can be, what is added. Clearly only a
fool or a madman would think they could add anything
poetically to Baudelaire, say, or Verlaine. But Molière, or,
to take another glaring example, Rostand – and I'd even
say Corneille, in the comedies – are different kettles of
fish. Molière, and the young Corneille were first and
foremost an *hommes de théâtre*, not poets. Consequently,
the verse translator (I personally feel there is no point in
translating French verse comedies into prose) may feel

39

they have something to bring to the poetic party here. There is, indeed, a thirty or more year tradition of British translators doing, or trying to do, just that, from Tony Harrison's groundbreaking version of *Le Misanthrope* (1973) onwards. Among those who have followed in Harrison's footsteps are: Martin Crimp, with his brilliant version of the same play; Liz Lockhead, with her virtuosic Scottish dialect translations (transformations might be a better word for these sorts of translation) of *L'Ecole des Femmes* and *Tartuffe*; my own efforts in this area; and so on. The nub of it is that whatever is being lost in such translations (if indeed anything is at all) it is not poetry, or at any rate not *great* poetry. Molière, and Corneille when he has his comic hat on, are writing in a lower genre – what would be better termed comic verse than poetry. Therein lies the long leash that their translators can allow themselves, the scope for licence and invention.

In a sense we have now come full circle back to Dryden, only modifying and refining his rule in the process. It's almost a mathematical question, a pure matter of ratios. If Dryden, himself a great poet, allows himself a *degree* of latitude with another great poet such as Virgil or Ovid, then we infinitely lesser lights, may allow ourselves some *licence* with a lesser poet like Molière, or Corneille in non-tragic, non-sublime mode. (His tragedies, like Racine's, would need a Dryden to do them poetic justice.)

In the realm of prose, the same rule – let's call it modified Dryden – applies: the lesser the author, the greater the permissible degree of freedom. Thus, going down the scale from top to bottom, it could be convincingly argued that one should not tamper at all with the greatest plays of Sophocles, say, or Ibsen, or Chekhov, or Goldoni, or Feydeau, but that a writer such as Marivaux, or a lesser play by, I don't know, Goldoni again, might well be regarded, at the risk of sounding outrageous, not to say arrogant, as "fair game". One might argue the toss about which playwrights and/or plays fit into which category, but that the categories at any rate do exist is, I would submit, not itself contentious. The principle, is a valid one. If I have been applying it to plays here, it works equally well for poetry and the novel, and what it amounts to is that one is as likely to betray a text by handling it with kid gloves, as by trampling all over it. Only, be careful which texts you handle in which way!

3. Lost in Translation

THE RUSSIAN LINGUIST and literary theorist Roman Jakobson maintained that poetry was, by definition, untranslatable. It has also, of course, been (famously) observed (and I've already quoted) that "poetry is what is lost in translation." I would like to modify this, while basically agreeing.

I've already looked at Dryden and Pope as translators, but in a different context. Then I was considering the principles and theory of translation as a whole. Another thing to bear in mind is that, as blank verse poets, of a more or less transparent type – by which I mean, not laden with dense imagery – both Homer and Virgil are, on a technical level, relatively easy poets to translate.

I've also already talked, in the context both of theatrical and poetic translation, about the importance of knowing who you're dealing with. The, as one might call it, "league table", Leavisite approach to literature may not be a particularly palatable one for everybody – certainly not these days, when political correctness has wormed its way into arts criticism, and one is barely allowed to assert that Tolstoy is, absolutely and indisutably, a better writer than Jilly Cooper – that it is all a matter of taste. Nevertheless, if somebody maintains that Warhol is as good an artist as Van Gough, it is important to be able to say – to *know* – that while they are entitled to hold that view (though they might want to seek professional help) they are, notwithstanding, quite simply, *wrong*. And the same goes for literature. We may quibble about who belongs to which league, boundaries may be blurred between the bottom of one and the top of the next, but that the leagues exist, and that a good many of the members of each are clear cut and not up for debate, is not merely an indisputable truth, but an essential one. Dispense with it, and the game of culture is not worth the candle. Many years ago a debate about this issue had flared up for some reason, and I was interviewed about it on *Newsnight*. The next speaker was the late Malcolm Bradbury, a writer I have long admired. When they put the same question to him, I felt not merely chuffed on a personal level, but immensely relieved, on a cultural one, when he began his remarks with: "I totally agree with what the previous speaker has just said."

Well, when it comes to translation, this reactionary approach can have its uses, and, indeed, translatability, or lack of it, can sometimes play its own, important role in deciding who belongs where. And this is particularly, nay, as we have said, *proverbially*, true of poetry. As a rule of thumb, the better a poet is, the less translatable.

On a sliding scale, then: if Baudelaire is untranslatable, even by a genius, Molière is eminently *trans*latable, by a practitioner with sufficient skill. Richard Wilbur has proved this with his wonderfully accurate and yet at the same time eminently speakable, playable, and witty translations of Molière, who, as I've already said, is in no way, shape or form a major poet. I would imagine that if Wilbur turned his hand to Corneille and Racine, with their dense rhetoric packed into taut, sonorous, sinuous Alexandrines, even he would have his work cut out.

At the other end of the scale, to pluck another name out of the air, even to attempt to translate Mallarmé would, in my view, be absurd. He's elusive and dense and difficult enough for a French reader to grasp, let alone for an English translator to render. A version of *L'Après-Midi d'un Faune* would, I respectfully submit be, analytically, *a priori*, a pointless exercise.

Leaving this rather bleak perspective to one side, and assuming that there are fools about who are ready to rush in where angels fear to tread, what are the guidelines? Verlaine's famous poetic dictum: "de la musique avant toute chose" certainly comes into the frame. If there are beautiful sonic textures such as assonance and alliteration in the original, then the translator should do his best to replicate them. Here he may have certain advantages. Many languages seem to be naturally alliterative, and in my view English is one of them. So an English translator, at any rate, has something to work with on the musical front.

Let me illustrate this with an effort of my own – a translation of Verlaine's *Le Faune:*

Le Faune

    Un vieux faune de terre cuite
    Rit au centre des boulingrins,
    Présageant sans doute une suite
    Mauvaise à ces instants sereins

    Qui m'ont conduit et t'ont conduite
    Mélancoliques pèlerins,
    Jusqu'à cette heure dont la fuite
    Tournoie au son des tambourins.

Literal translation:

    An old terracotta faun is laughing in the middle of the greensward, presaging, without doubt, dire future events to follow these serene moments that have brought me and have brought you, melancholy pilgrims, to this hour whose flight turns whirls round to the sound of the tambourines.

The Faun

An old terracotta faun
Is laughing on the green
And somehow seems to warn
Of threats to the serene

Moments that took us two
Sad pilgrims to this hour
Whose flight goes whirling to
The tapping of the tambour.

This comes quite close on a certain, limited level. Perhaps most importantly, it maintains the form: the meter is regular, if not identical to Verlaine's, and my version also follows the rhyme-scheme. Such formal fidelity is absolutely essential, in my opinion – no, not in my opinion, but irrefutably – in the translation of poetry. My effort also manages to replicate the *musique* (by introducing a decent dose of alliteration) and it is faithful to the imagery – the signifiers, to use a technical term, are accurately reproduced. And yet it is still far from Verlaine. And Verlaine, mark you, is a more translatable poet than many. He is not transparent, like Homer or Virgil, or Dante, but neither is he taxing, like Mallarmé, or Baudelaire, or Eliot. When you get to a poem like *L'Après-Midi d'Un Faun,* already mentioned, or, to take another symbolist example, Valéry's *Le Cimetière Marin,* the task of keeping all the, so to speak, poetic balls in the air becomes impossible, or that, at any rate, is my hunch. (I have, in fact, done a version of *Le Cimetière.* It was a creditable attempt, but all the exercise really achieved, in the end, was to remind me how impossible to translate some poets, or poems, are.)

Then there are other poems whose musicality is so magical it is impossible to imagine anyone, other than, perhaps, another great poet, coming close to producing a translation, in any meaningful sense of the word. Virgil and Homer have elements of that, now I think of it, but the music is not *so* much of the equation as to make the exercise of translating them one hundred per cent futile. On the other hand, when you consider a (more or less transparent, yet sublimely musical) poet like Petrarch, you begin to wonder why anyone would bother. Consider just the opening quatrain of *Rime Sparse.* I think, even without knowing Italian, if you heard the following lines read out loud, by an Italian, or someone versed in the language, you would be entranced simply by the *sounds* the words make:

> Voi ch'ascoltat' in rime sparse il suono
> Di quei sospiri ond' io nodriva il cuore

In sul mio primo giovenil' errore
Quand' ero in part' altr' om' da qual che sono.

This is as good as sonic virtuosity gets in poetry. An equivalent in English would be, say, Oberon's great speech in *A Midsummer Night's Dream* – "I know a bank…" Anyone who attempted to translate that would, in my opinion, have to be either insane, or else themselves a poet of immense talent. If you're not convinced yet, I would invite you to perform a quick thought experiment. Think of a poem – let's say… *The Wasteland*… and then imagine a French or German translation of it. It need not necessarily be a disaster, but so much of the tonal texture; the resonance of many of the allusions, which are to English literature; the music and rhythm – all this would be lost.

A final thought about formal correspondence. I believe this is necessary, as I have already suggested. It would, quite patently, be pointless to translate Baudelaire, Verlaine, Leopardi, whoever, into blank verse, or prose. But this is also true of Molière's major verse plays. The couplet form is germane to the experience, and also to the ethos. Imagine watching a translation of the wonderful scenes in which Tartuffe attempts to seduce Elmire, not played in couplets. It would be like eating meringues without the sugar. However, if replication, or some approximation to it, of form is necessary, it is most certainly *not* sufficient. Take this example – a clutch of translations of the Persian poet Sa'di's *Oneness of Mankind:*

Literal version:

All men are members of the same body,
Created from one essence.
If fate brings suffering to one member,
The others cannot stay at rest.
You who remain indifferent
To the burden of pain of others,
Do not deserve to be called human.

Translations:

All Adam's sons are limbs of one another,
Each of the self same substance as his brother.
So while one member suffers aches and grief,
The other members cannot win relief.
Thou, who are heedless of thy brother's pain,
It is not right at all to name thee man.
A. J. Arberry

Human beings are members of a whole,
In creation of one essence and soul.
If one member is afflicted with pain,
Other members uneasy will remain.

If you have no sympathy for human pain,
The name of human you cannot retain.
M. Aryanpoor

Adam's sons are body limbs, to say;
For they're created of the same clay.
Should one organ be troubled by pain,
Others would suffer severe strain.
Thou careless of people's suffering,
Deserve not the name, 'human being'.
H. Vahid Dastjerdi

In these versions meter is employed ineptly, word orders are comically contorted and unidiomatic, and the rhymes whine at us like a swarm of potter-wasps. If ever we needed proof that a good translator of poetry should, ideally, be a poet himself, then these versions provide it. They are all, self-evidently, bad. You may think I am talking my book here – picking an aunt sally to prove a point about the literary translation of poetry, but I suspect not. I suspect that the fact that no fewer than three professional translators have taken on the same poem – thrown themselves at the same fence, so to speak – and fallen, is evidence of something fundamental: the inherent untranslatability of poetry.

4. Benjamin: Above And Beyond

WALTER BENJAMIN'S FAMOUS essay – the most read and discussed of all examinations of the nature of translation – *The Task of the Translator* – itself a mass of often (at any rate to this reader) incomprehensible (maybe untranslatable?) concept-weaving, has had so much additional abstraction written about it that, despite one's initial, Anglo-Saxon scepticism, one feels it must be worth persevering with, that it contains, with luck, at least one or two nuggets of truth. In that respect it quite closely resembles a religious text, and indeed its language is, somewhat irritatingly, suffused with quasi-Cabbalistic undertones. As with theologians on the scriptures, one's instinct tells one, so with intellectuals on this essay, surely so many good minds would not have expended so much of their own time, and occupied so much of ours, for no reason at all?

After wading through the mire of – one is tempted to say tendentious – verbiage, but let's leave it at unverifiable conceptualizing – that trips off Benjamin's pen with such consummate, hoodwinking ease, I emerged with one important truth in my hand. If I have read him right, then his essay could be said to take me right back to my preface, and the inferiority complex I discovered myself to be suffering from when my friend ran down my status as a translator in front of that girl at the Groucho Club.

For Benjamin, the task of the translator is not an entirely inferior one. On the contrary, it has its own, exalted place in the literary and linguistic scheme of things. The inherent untranslatability of great literature, Benjamin argues (assuming I have understood him correctly – and, if you haven't read him, believe me, that is no mean feat in itself) is not a negative, but rather something to be embraced and accepted. The role of the translator is not to render something (what Benjamin calls an "intention", but we might prefer to call a "meaning" – the paraphrasable content I spoke about at the start of this book) but to carry the family of languages a step further toward an ultimate, an exalted, even mystical goal – a unity, in which meaning almost disappears. That goal of taking language back to a pre-Babelesque purity – every good translation is a step along that path, a rung in that ladder – enables us translators to think rather better of ourselves than we did before. Everywhere our function is described in the loftiest terms. We "point the way...in a singularly impressive manner...to the hitherto inaccessible realm of reconciliation and fulfilment of languages." To reach this goal would be finally to pass beyond what Mallarmé calls "The imperfection of languages" which "consists in their plurality; the supreme one is lacking: thinking is writing without accessories, or even whispering, the immortal word remains silent; the diversity of idioms on earth prevents everybody from uttering that which otherwise, at a single stroke, would materialize as truth."

Thanks to Benjamin, then – always assuming you buy into the theorizing, and many critics do – we translators would seem to have acquired a new importance. Now I've read Benjamin's essay, the next time a sexy actress asks me what I do, I won't say: "I'm a translator." I shall tell her that I "put the hallowed growth of languages to the test." It'll sound a lot cooler, I reckon, even if she may not have a clue what I mean.

Benjamin is apt, unsurprisingly, to overstate his case and mis-speak in the process. He still cleaves, implicitly, to the notion of some inherent inferiority, qua craft, of translation to writing, rendition to "creation", and the distinction appears to be a blanket one. At one point, for instance, he writes that "translation, unlike art, cannot claim permanence for its products." Again, translation is said to signify a "more exalted language than its own." If this is meant across the board, then it is patently absurd. Pope's Homer will be read for as long as Homer himself – likewise with Dryden and Virgil, or Marlowe's masterly renditions of Ovid's elegies – and those are just three randomly selected examples from one language. As for Molière, I would humbly submit that he has been extremely fortunate to have his rather ordinary verse, his not particularly witty French, rendered by the likes of Tony Harrison and myself into sparkling, comically inventive English. Apart from anything else – and if I have already made this point then it is worth repeating – English is a language which, when rhymed, lends itself far more readily to humour than French. If not, it's worth reminding the reader how English rhymes – particularly monosyllabic, Anglo-Saxon ones such as "quirk/berk"; "clog/dog", and so on, contribute comedy in themselves, in addition to rendering Benjamin's "intention". This, I suspect, is one reason why Michael Frayn said of my version of *Le Menteur* that it was a better play in English than it had been in French, and the same has doubtless been said of Martin Crimp's and Tony Harrison's brilliant versions of *Le Misanthrope,* and of Richard Wilbur's virtuoso renditions of Molière's verse comedies.

I emerged from my reading of Benjamin's essay, with a wet towel over my head, yes, but feeling better about myself and what I have been doing for the past twenty years, and what my fellow literary translators will be doing until literature ceases to be written. There will always be bad ones, certainly, and the good ones will slip up from time to time, as I have done myself many a time and oft – as, for example, with my catastrophic rendition of the

Oedipus plays for Peter Hall's production at the National Theatre, but our calling, thanks to Benjamin, has been revealed to be a nobler one than many people, and perhaps we ourselves, might have thought.

Notes

1. Reviewing my version of *Tartuffe* on the BBC's Late Review, 1991.

2. John Dryden, *To The Earl of Roscomon, on his Excellent Essay on Translated Verse*, ll 30 – 38.

3. John Dryden, Preface to *Fables Ancient and Modern*, ll 585 – 587.

4. John Dryden, Preface to *Fables Ancient and Modern*, ll 557 – 559.

5. Alexander Pope, Preface to his translation of *The Iliad*, 1715.

6. Gilles Ménage (1615–1692) commenting on the translations of Nicolas Perrot d'Ablancourt.

7. Homer, *Iliad*, Book 23 l 613.

8. Homer, *Iliad*, ll 704-5.

9. Pope, *Iliad*, ll 818-19.

10. Virgil, *Aeneid*, l.3.

11. Dryden, *Aeneid*, ll.3-4.

12. "He enlarged very convincingly upon the excellence of rhyme over blank verse in English poetry." Boswell, *Life of Johnson*, AD 1763.

13. *Arturo Ui*, Royal National Theatre, 1991, dir. Di Trevis. One member of the cast, who shall remain nameless, lost his only big speech in the bloodbath that followed the first preview. He was, to say the least, not pleased.

14. *Tartuffe*, Act IV, Scene Five, ll 71-2.

15. Corneille, *Le Menteur*, III.3. 907-909.

16. Jeremy Kingston reviewing *The Sisterhood* in The Times, November, 1987. (I prefer to forget the precise date.)

17. Charles Spencer reviewing *Tartuffe* in the Daily Telegraph, February 19th, 2002.